Enjoy!!
Happy Birthday —
Neil + Pam

NEW ENGLAND COAST

PHOTOGRAPHY BY WILLIAM HUBBELL

CAPTIONS BY JEAN M. HUBBELL

FOREWORD BY JAMES RUSSELL WIGGINS

GRAPHIC ARTS CENTER PUBLISHING COMPANY, PORTLAND, OREGON

To Pare Lorentz (1906-1992)
A defender of nature's beauty,
a poet with words and film,
a teacher and a friend.

International Standard Book Number 1-55868-100-0
Library of Congress Number 92-70119
© MCMXCII by Graphic Arts Center Publishing Company
P.O. Box 10306 • Portland, Oregon 97210
No part of this book may be reproduced by any means
without the permission of the publisher.
President • Charles M. Hopkins
Editor-in-Chief • Douglas A. Pfeiffer
Managing Editor • Jean Andrews
Designer • Robert Reynolds
Typographer • Harrison Typesetting, Inc.
Color Separations • Agency Litho
Printer • Dynagraphics, Inc.
Bindery • Lincoln & Allen
Printed in the United States of America

◄ ◄ Schooners (and spectators!) approach the finish line in Rockland, Maine's annual Windjammer Race. Stately coasting schooners, such as the three-masted *Victory Chimes,* once plied the coast of New England, carrying their wares "Down East" from the busy harbors of Boston and New York. ◄ The West Quoddy Head lighthouse in Lubec was built in 1791 on the easternmost point of land in the United States. Its striped tower houses a powerful light and foghorn to warn sailors of the treacherous shores of Passamaquoddy Bay. With fifty-foot tides in the adjacent Bay of Fundy in New Brunswick, the area has been studied by scientists regarding tidal electrical power generation.

FOREWORD

The rugged New England coast, as seen through the camera lenses of great photographers like William Hubbell, appeals to two audiences— those who have seen it and wish to recapture it and those who have not seen it and like to see in print what they hope to see in person.

It is a special coast culture, all of which differs from that anywhere else in America and parts of which differ from each other, in a way that delights and surprises. It is a fair object of examination by photographers whose appreciation is something more than a visual sensation, who have taken the pains to know the life beyond the looks and who make their selections in a way that captures something of that life. That is what Hubbell did with his marvelous book on Connecticut; and that is what he has done on this larger screen, NEW ENGLAND COAST.

Those who have seen much of the New England Coast many times will get from this book the pleasant sensation that comes when you once again meet an old and familiar friend. We cannot stay the alterations of age in the people we know or in the places we know, but the camera can do that, conferring a kind of immortality on the places we have known and loved. That's what William Hubbell's lenses do for those with long-remembered views of life along the bays, inlets, and streams of New England.

JAMES RUSSELL WIGGINS
Former Editor, *Washington Post*

▲ Navigation is tricky for all manner of yachtsmen in Jonesport, Maine. Sailing skippers called their easterly journey from Boston to Maine harbors "sailing Down East" because the prevailing southwest winds pushed them before the wind to their eastern destinations without strenuous tacking upwind. This stretch of coastline is framed by dark spruce and fir—although often obscured by fog.
▶ Across Moosabec Reach (known as "Moose a' Becky's Beach" in 1770) from Jonesport is Beals Island. The area is home to one of Maine's fastest and largest fleets of lobster boats. Annual lobster boat races provide summer diversion for hardworking fishermen.

◄ Maine's Washington County, nicknamed "Sunrise County," is the first place in the continental United States to see the sun. It contains more than two hundred thousand acres of blueberry barrens. Lanes marked with twine assist harvesters using scooped, forklike "rakes." More than sixty million pounds of blueberries are marketed yearly.
▲ Traditionally, popovers and tea are served—with a view of The Bubbles—at Jordan Pond House on Maine's Mount Desert Island. In 1604, Samuel de Champlain named it "L'Isle des Monts Déserts" for its barren mountains. Mount Desert, home of Acadia National Park, is the largest rock-based island on the Atlantic Coast.

Under the high mountains of the Penobscot,
against whose feet the sea doth beat.
CAPTAIN JOHN SMITH

▲ Surrounded by nature's glory, worshippers sing at sunset vespers atop Cadillac Mountain in Maine's Acadia National Park. This 1,530-foot, glacier-smoothed granite peak was named for Antoine de la Mothe Cadillac, the founder of Detroit, and can be climbed by hikers and automobiles alike. Acadia, one of America's most popular national parks, greets more than four million tourists annually.
▶ Bass Harbor Marsh in Acadia National Park is exemplary of a salt marsh. These seaside wetlands, created when barrier beaches block fresh water drainage, provide nurturing environments for marine life and for more than three hundred species of birds.

*The tints of autumn—a mighty flower garden
blossoming under the spell of the enchanter, Frost.*
JOHN GREENLEAF WHITTIER

◄ Canoeists near Mount Desert Island's Bar Harbor enjoy a leisurely paddle on an Indian summer afternoon. Maine boasts several thousand lakes and rivers that offer smooth- or white-water canoeists endless variety. Tourism ranks a close second to Maine's paper industry in total revenue. The Bar Harbor area—once the enclave of millionaires such as J. P. Morgan and John D. Rockefeller who lived in elegant "cottages"—remains popular today with vacationers.
▲ Limpid, luminous pre-dawn *chiaroscuro* (light and dark) reflects in a tidal pool on Great Cranberry Island. Mussels found in such pools provide sustenance for humans, starfish, crabs, and sea gulls. The Cranberry Isles, along with more than two thousand coastal islands, are home to fishermen, summer folk, and marine life.

Under the shoulder of 940-foot-high Blue Hill, one of Maine's prominent coastal landmarks, the century-old Blue Hill Fair marks the end of summer. Author E. B. White, a long-time area resident, may well have had this old-fashioned country fair in mind when he wrote the children's favorite, *Charlotte's Web*. Traditional events such as oxen pulls, livestock and agricultural exhibits, and sheepdog trials mingle with the sights and sounds of the midway. Sheep farmers abounded in Maine in the nineteenth century and found Maine's islands ideal corrals for their stock.

Oh, what a blamed uncertain thing
this pesky weather is!
It blew and snew and then it thew
And now, by jing, it's friz!
PHILANDER JOHNSON

◄ The abundant, superior-quality pink granite that underlies Deer Isle, Maine, forms many of Stonington's fishing wharves. Beginning in the nineteenth century, granite, quarried from the adjacent Crotch Island, was shipped by schooner and railroad to build the Library of Congress, the Cape Cod Canal, the George Washington Bridge, and the Rockefeller Center. The quarry still operates today.
▲ Seagulls circle a fishing boat at a sardine cannery in Stonington's busy, working harbor. Herring gulls dive for scraps from the fishing fleet. Visible through the rain and fog of a September storm are several of the spruce-fringed, granite islands in Merchants' Row. Accessible only by boat, these islands epitomize Maine's beauty.

*All I could see from where I stood
was three long mountains and a wood.*
EDNA ST. VINCENT MILLAY

▲Dawn spreads over Penobscot Bay, seen from Mount Battie in Maine's Camden Hills. The view inspired Edna St. Vincent Millay to write her poem "Renascence." Penobscot Bay's many islands—actually submerged mountain peaks—buffer the ocean's force and make the bay a haven for sailors. Thirteen thousand years ago, Ice Age glaciers carved peninsulas and points to depths of over a mile.
▶ In the shadow of an old schoolhouse, low-bush wild blueberries bloom on land that slopes down to Eggemoggin Reach, which separates Deer Isle from the mainland.

◄ Its summit draped with a crimson mantle of autumn blueberry barrens, Caterpillar Hill in Sedgwick, Maine, sweeps clear down to Penobscot Bay. Among the world's best cruising grounds, the Bay is home to multimasted charter schooners called windjammers.
▲ An April snow frosts the peaks of Cadillac and Sargent mountains on Mount Desert, and dusts the Cranberry Isles. An old saying warns, "If you don't like the weather, wait a minute!" Although the vagaries of its weather are legend, Maine offers sparkling sunshine for over sixty percent of the year, while coastal communities may receive up to seventy inches of snow per year. Cradled to the left of the mountains is Somes Sound, the only true glacial fjord on the East Coast of the United States.

▲ A classic lapstrake wooden boat waits reflectively for an outing. Maine's wooden shipbuilding industry flourished in the 1800s, and local craftsmen uphold the tradition even today in many coastal villages where these wooden boats are still produced. ▶ Stacked on a Port Clyde dock, lobster traps form a colorful pattern. This working harbor, home to lobstermen and draggers alike, is a departure point for Monhegan Island's mailboat. Traditional, rounded wooden-slat lobster pots are slowly being replaced by more durable—and stackable—wire traps. Maine has more than three thousand full-time lobstermen who land approximately twenty-three million pounds each year. This seafood delicacy— bottle green or blue when alive—is enjoyed by diners worldwide.

◄ The coastal forest, which crowds right down to Maine's rock-bound shore, embraces deciduous hardwood trees—like this clump of white birch—and conifers such as spruce and pine. Commercial forestry remains the state's largest industry and provides employment for approximately one-tenth of Maine's one million citizens.
▲ Twilight softens the panorama that includes Camden Harbor on the left, Rockport Harbor to the upper right, and Owl's Head on the horizon. Camden's scenic, snug setting, lovely homes, and bustling village make it a popular vacation destination by land or sea. Rockport is another favorite harbor, home for many years to André, the trained Maine harbor seal. In the 1800s, Rockport was the center of Maine's lime industry, and several old kilns remain.

I'll tell you how the Sun rose—A Ribbon at a time.
EMILY DICKINSON

▲ A fishing trawler breaks the calm water just west of Islesboro in Maine's Penobscot Bay. Islesboro has many elegant, vintage summer "cottages." Year-round islanders sometimes had mixed feelings about people "from away," as reported by Michael Kinnecutt: "A solitary fisherman was setting out his nets, when a private steam yacht dropped anchor a ways out. Someone waved the fisherman over. He rowed across. A fancy fellow climbed into the boat and told the fisherman to take him ashore, 'My name is George Washington Childe Drexel, and I just bought that land and intend to build a large house with stables.' The fisherman squarely regarded the passenger and replied, 'My name is George Robeson, and this is my punt.'"
▶ Traditional windjammers and contemporary schooners boil along during the annual July race from Vinalhaven to Rockland.

◄ Whiling away a foggy morning in Vinalhaven, Maine, is serious business, requiring great concentration. Ferry service connects Carver's Harbor on the island with the mainland at Rockland. Vinalhaven was an important granite quarrying location. In the 1890s, four 360-ton columns were cut and shipped from Carver's Harbor for the altar of New York's Cathedral of St. John the Divine. ▲ A trawler rides the early morning tide past Owl's Head Light into Rockland Harbor. More lobsters are packed and shipped in Rockland than anywhere else in the world. Blue Hill breaks the horizon in the center distance. The Farnsworth Museum in the town of Rockland contains work by three generations of Wyeth painters.

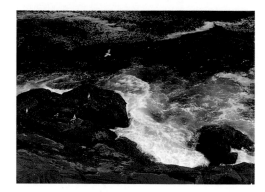

Monhegan Island's rugged, 160-foot-high cliffs are the highest on the East Coast. This mile-square island's beauty and isolation have long been a magnet for artists and nature-lovers alike. Cathedral Woods, in the island's center, is a magical and majestic evergreen forest carpeted with mosses. Careful searches may even reveal fairy houses! Behind the hotel is Manana Island, where it is said eleventh-century Norse explorers scratched their runes into the rocks. Mailboat service from Port Clyde and from Boothbay Harbor connects Monhegan to the mainland, visible ten miles in the distance. Maine's name perhaps originated from fishermen who sought to differentiate offshore islands from the "main" land.

*What makes Monhegan different
is that it's hard to get to and hard to live on,
and anything that makes it easier
is a step in the wrong direction.*
MONHEGAN ISLANDER—ANONYMOUS

◄ The path to the Monhegan Island ferry landing weaves between
a weathered cottage and the island's hotel garden. Meeting the
mailboat is a daily highlight. In 1524, Giovanni da Verrazzano
put in at Monhegan Island during his search for a route to China.
▲ The Bath Iron Works' crane—the western hemisphere's tallest—
looms over the traditional spires and roofs of this historic shipbuilding city on the banks of Maine's Kennebec River, which flows
150 miles from its source in Moosehead Lake. In 1607, early English
settlers founded the short-lived Popham Colony at the mouth of
the Kennebec. Bath's maritime heritage dates from the eighteenth
century, when over one-third of the British merchant fleet was
American-built. This tradition is well-preserved in the old sea
captains' homes and at the Maine Maritime Museum.

The sky is the daily bread of the eyes.
RALPH WALDO EMERSON

▲ The Cuckolds Light stands at the end of Cape Newagen, Maine. The Sheepscot River, background for author Rachel Carson in *The Sea Around Us*, lies to the west, and the resort, Boothbay Harbor, to the east. Incoming "mackerel sky" promises a less benign day.
▶ The Pemaquid Light stands like a solitary sentinel watching the moonrise. Lighthouses are part of the basic essence of the New England Coast. Once tended by keepers whose heroic rescue efforts inspired poets and artists, all are now totally automated. Rocky Muscongus Bay is just around the corner from Pemaquid Point. The bay's Eastern Egg Rock hosts a rare puffin nesting colony.

NOTICE
SURROUNDING PARK AREA
NOT UNDER CONTROL OF
THE COAST GUARD
AND THE COAST GUARD IS NOT
RESPONSIBLE FOR ITS OPERATION

◄ Although Wiscasset—whose name means "meeting of three tides"—hugs the west bank of the Sheepscot River some fourteen miles upstream from the open sea, it was once the busiest clipper ship port in Maine. Cargoes of lumber and ice were shipped worldwide by schooners such as the *Luther Little* and the *Hesper*, whose hulks lie alongside the waterfront of Wiscasset.
▲ The winter winds sweep roiling clouds across Littlejohn Island, one of Casco Bay's "Calendar Islands"—which reputedly number 365. Just north lie the Harraseeket River and Freeport, home of world-famous retailer L. L. Bean. Mast Landing, on the river, was a depot for British Royal Navy mast trees cut from Maine's huge pines.

▲ The only cribwork bridge in the world connects the Casco Bay islands of Orr's and Bailey. The filigree granite slabs, laid without cement, allow free tidal flow. West of Bailey Island is Eagle Island, where Admiral Robert E. Peary built his summer home by the bay.
▶ Maine's Androscoggin River Falls once provided the power for this textile mill located where Topsham meets Brunswick. Also in Brunswick, Bowdoin College, founded in 1794, typifies the excellent education available at New England's many private colleges.

Portland, at Casco Bay's entrance, is Maine's largest city, but, with a population under seventy thousand, it combines the charm of a small town with the cultural and commercial advantages of larger cities. Originally named Falmouth, Portland began as a fishing and timbering seaport. The Old Port Exchange area now houses restaurants and shops in nineteenth-century brick warehouses and classic Victorian mansions built after the devastating fire of 1866. Many of Casco Bay's islands are populated by year-round and summer residents. Boating of all kinds is a popular activity, and an island power plant also serves as a sailors' landmark.

▲ Portland Head Light looks peaceful and serene on a midsummer evening, but its light marks a treacherous, unforgiving shoreline. Commissioned in 1791 by George Washington, the lighthouse was constructed of the local fieldstone. Its three-hundred-thousand-candlepower light alerts vessels up to sixteen miles out at sea.
▶ A snowstorm's heavy surf batters rocks on the exposed point at Cape Elizabeth's Two Lights State Park. The cape's twin lights once helped ships differentiate the point from Portland Head, although one light is now abandoned. Coastal marine plants that have developed in these rocky climes have adapted to extremes of temperature, tidal turbulence, and pounding surf.

◄ In Ogunquit, Maine, the Old Perkins Place, which began as a log cabin, has been inhabited by members of the Perkins family since 1719. Everything necessary for daily living was either bartered for or raised. Isaiah Perkins, who lived here at the turn of the century, was grateful when summer people began coming to the area, because occupations related to tourism gave him a more reliable and less strenuous way to earn a living than traditional fishing and farming.

▲ Marginal Way overlooks Ogunquit, a word which means the "beautiful place by the sea." Beaches make up only sixty miles of Maine's thirty-five hundred miles of coastline. Created by a combination of wind, waves, tides, and storms, they are continually in a changing process. Ogunquit's fine beach is classified as a barrier spit, and its sand dunes help protect the beach from erosion.

▲ With stabilizing sail furled, a lobster boat returns to the tiny harbor at Perkins Cove, Maine. This manmade harbor was dredged in 1941 at the spot where the Josias River flows into Oarweed Cove.
► Cape Neddick Light, on The Nubble in York, has welcomed mariners to Maine waters since 1879. A Pilgrim trading post called "Agamenticus" was the forerunner of York, and historic buildings still face the common in this coastal community.

◄ Dressed in early American garb, this girl re-lives colonial times at Strawbery Banke in Portsmouth, New Hampshire. Craftsmen—coopers, weavers, smiths—practice traditional trades in restored shops. At some locations, historians and archaeologists allow visitors to participate vicariously in the ongoing restoration process.

▲ Strawbery Banke is an outdoor museum. Historic homes and shops have been preserved and restored in the city's waterfront Puddle Dock neighborhood. English colonists in 1630 found abundant wild strawberries covering the banks of the Piscataqua River and named their community accordingly. The seventeenth-century Sherburne House, seen here after an autumn snowfall, is the oldest of the Puddle Dock homes. Period flower, herb, and vegetable gardens add to visitors' knowledge of colonial life.

Who loves a garden still his Eden keeps,
Perennial pleasures plants, and wholesome harvest reaps.
AMOS ALCOTT

▲ Portsmouth, New Hampshire, enjoyed its heyday during the eighteenth and nineteenth centuries. Sea captains and merchants built fine Georgian homes along the harbor's quay. Many, like the yellow Wentworth-Gardner house, are embellished with intricately carved wooden paneling and moldings. To symbolize hospitality, sea captains, returning home from safe voyages, placed a pineapple outside their door to invite friends to share in refreshments.
▶ New Hampshire meets the sea at just eighteen miles of sandy coastline. Inland from the beaches, the state's rolling glacial topography and fertile soils nourish fruit farms such as this six-hundred-acre orchard in Hampton Falls. Year-round care—such as pruning, cultivating, and fertilizing of the twenty thousand apple trees—yields a bountiful crop in the fall.

REV. NATHANIEL ROGERS, W
than 47 years, a faithful & belov
r of the first Church & Congreg
lace. Colleague the first 18 years

Ye marshes, how candid and simply
and nothing-withholding and free
Ye publish yourselves to the sky
And offer yourselves to the sea!
SIDNEY LANIER

◄ Ipswich, one of the oldest towns in Massachusetts, has the greatest number of seventeenth-century Puritan dwellings in the country. Graves of early settlers can be found in the Old Burial Ground. As a child, Salem native Nathaniel Hawthorne, the author of *The House of the Seven Gables,* frequently stopped at the headstone of Reverend Rogers in order to count the parson's buttons!
▲ Salt marshes are common in the area around Newbury, along the banks of the Merrimac River. These tidal marshes provided colonists with salt hay for cattle feed and for stable bedding. Today, marsh hay is harvested for use as garden mulch.

▲ Castle Hill is located high above Crane's Beach on Massachusetts' North Shore. This magnificent estate, formerly home of plumbing millionaire Richard Crane, is now run by a non-profit foundation which sponsors summer concerts on the well-manicured grounds.
► The Whipple House, built in 1640, shows the diversity of Ipswich architecture. This Elizabethan-style house, which remained in the Whipple family for more than two hundred years, is now the home of the Ipswich Historical Society.

◄ Rockport Harbor is on the eastern coast of Cape Ann, some thirty-five miles north of Boston, Massachusetts. Rockport became a busy nineteenth-century shipping center for granite which was quarried on nearby Halibut Point. The point was named not for the fish, but rather in reference to the sailing term, "haul about."
▲ Villagers and visitors enjoy Rockport's annual Independence Day Firemen's Parade, which welcomes the creative participation of all.

▲ Salem, Massachusetts, is known for its seventeenth-century witchcraft trials, its eighteenth-century merchant shipping, and its nineteenth-century manufacturing. A gilded eagle tops the Custom House, which stands at the head of Derby Wharf, the Revolutionary base of some one hundred fifty patriot privateers responsible for the demise of more than four hundred British ships.
▶ The struggle for American independence was nurtured in Boston. Paul Revere, shown here astride his bronzed horse, made his legendary ride to Lexington to alert the Minutemen after a two-lantern signal was hung in the steeple of the adjacent Old North Church. These historic sites are among those in the Boston National Historical Park, known as the Freedom Trail.

◄ An impressive arch at Rowe's Wharf on Boston Harbor fronts a contemporary hotel-office complex. Boston's maritime history peaked in the 1800s when clipper ships abounded, but the waterfront later declined until modern restoration projects injected new vitality into this area of the city. Today, commercial, maritime, and cultural interests combine to make the waterfront an exciting place.
▲ Boston's Public Garden is a favorite place for walking and enjoying the outdoors, and a serene backdrop for a fall wedding. It is also famed for its graceful swan boats, and offers the respite of sweeping lawns and immaculate flower gardens. Boston retains a neighborhood intimacy and diversity uncommon in large cities. Its ethnically diverse population affords a mixture of nationalities, each retaining its own unique cultural characteristics.

The rocky nook with hilltops three
Looked eastward from the farms,
And twice each day the flowing sea
Took Boston in its arms.
RALPH WALDO EMERSON

▲ Of Boston's three original hills, the only one remaining is Beacon Hill. The others were flattened during the nineteenth century to provide landfill for the expanding city. Although dwarfed by the financial center, the dome of the State House, designed in 1795 by Charles Bulfinch, rises above the fashionable homes of its Beacon Hill neighbors. At the foot of the hill, the Charles River— Boston's Back Bay—brings water sports to Bostonians' doorsteps.
▶ A double rainbow arches over Duxbury Bay, south of Boston. Duxbury was settled in 1627, when Plymouth residents such as Myles Standish and John Alden searched for additional grazing land for their livestock. Duxbury's harbor, among others, was subsequently used by cod and mackerel fishing fleets.

Pilgrim Separatists landed in Plymouth, Massachusetts, in 1620, seeking religious freedom. This first permanent New England settlement is remembered at a variety of historic sites, which include Plymouth Rock, *Mayflower II* (an authentic replica of the original *Mayflower),* and Plimoth Plantation. Plimoth Plantation is a living museum, which re-creates the 1627 stockaded village. Costumed "Pilgrims" portray actual residents—including using Elizabethan accents. These interpreters will not slip out of character or out of century! Daily plantation life is reenacted, showing residents harvesting crops, baking, salting fish, and drilling with the militia.

▲ Cranberry bogs in coastal Massachusetts produce a large percentage of the world's crop. The berries—whose name originated because blossoms resemble a crane's head—thrive where sand abounds to cover the vines. Harvesting, once done manually, is now mechanized. Pumps retrieve the berries after they have been knocked loose from the vines by a water reel in the flooded bogs.
▶ The Old Ship Meetinghouse in Hingham has housed worshipping congregations continuously since 1681. Its roof was constructed utilizing curving oak frames such as those commonly used in shipbuilding. Workers erected its frame in only three days, after which they consumed nineteen barrels of hard cider!

Highland Light, or Cape Cod Light, atop windswept dunes in Truro, Massachusetts, was built in 1795 to warn seafaring vessels away from the treacherous sandbars that fringe Cape Cod. Even with such navigational aids, thousands of ships were wrecked during the 1800s off the eastern dunes of what is now the Cape Cod National Seashore. Brewster, where many prosperous sea captains built stately homes, is today a pleasant stop for summer visitors attracted by Cape Cod's beaches and its quaint, shingled cottages. The Bourne Farm has had only three owners since its construction in 1775. Built by yeoman Joseph Crowell, this farmstead and adjoining four buildings look today very much as they did when the property was one of only seven houses in West Falmouth. Salt Pond Sanctuary maintains this antique Cape Cod structure for the public.

A handful of sand is an anthology of the universe.
DAVID McCORD

▲ Martha's Vineyard, south of Cape Cod in Massachusetts, was named by Englishman Bartholomew Gosnold for his daughter and the island's abundant wild grapes. "The Vineyard" was an important whaling center and today is a summer resort. Menemsha Pond, site of a U.S. Coast Guard Station, is a busy fishing community. ▶ Variegated Gay Head Cliffs, over one hundred million years old, contain prehistoric animal fossils. Formerly known as Aquinnah, the town of Gay Head has a substantial population of Wampanoag Indians. This former Chief of the Tribal Council, sitting on Moshup's Beach, recently rallied the tribe. These Native Americans, descendants of those who helped the Pilgrims, sought the return of ancient tribal lands. Her message is, "We're still here."

◄ Farming the land and fishing the sea were the trades that occupied early New Englanders until the Industrial Revolution in the late eighteenth century. The fertile fields and pastures near Narragansett Bay on the Massachusetts coast were ideal for agriculture during the colonial period. Some saltwater farms still exist in Westport.
▲ New Bedford, famed whaling port and setting for *Moby Dick*, is the nation's number one fishing port in total revenue. Cobblestoned Centre Street, opposite the waterfront where modern scallopers and freighters unload cargoes, was at the center of New Bedford's golden age. The Waterfront Historic Area LeaguE, or WHALE, is instrumental in preserving and restoring this historic neighborhood where the lightship *New Bedford* is a nautical museum.

▲ The New England Coast is commonly divided into six regions: The drowned coastline of Down East Maine; the coastal plain of southern Maine and New Hampshire; the transitional Boston Basin; the terminal glacial moraines of Cape Cod and the islands; The Banks, underwater plateaus which stretch from New York to Newfoundland; and Long Island Sound. Common along the coast is the colorful *Rosa rugosa,* sometimes called the "seaside rose."

▶ Docked on the Taunton River banks in Fall River, Massachusetts, is the battleship USS *Massachusetts,* known as "Big Mamie." She took part in more than thirty-five World War II battles, firing salvos from her sixteen-inch guns. Six-story stone textile mills, seen just beyond the bridge, are reminiscent of Fall River's past as a producer of cotton thread and cloth. Today, they are factory outlet stores.

◄ Bristol, on Narragansett Bay, was an important Rhode Island harbor during the seventeenth and eighteenth centuries. The whole town gets involved in its Fourth of July parade, the nation's oldest, which has been held annually since 1785. Bristol is also the home of the Herreshoff boatyards where sleek America's Cup defenders and elegant steam yachts have been built for over a century.
▲ Along with the parade, local Bristol fire departments celebrate the Fourth with a water battle. Two teams of four men each—so heavily padded they must be carried onto the field—stand back-to-back. A fifth team member shouts instructions from the sidelines as the fire hoses shoot water at eighty pounds pressure.

▲ Providence was founded in 1636 by Roger Williams, who fled Massachusetts seeking religious tolerance. Prosperous seafaring merchants built homes on Benefit Street, widened "for the common benefit to all" to lessen congestion along the waterfront. More than one hundred homes such as William Snow's have been maintained or restored on Providence's "mile of history." Rhode Island's State House, seen beyond the houses, has the second-largest unsupported marble dome in the world, after St. Peter's, in Rome.
▶ Pawtucket—"place by a waterfall"—is considered the birthplace of the Industrial Revolution in the United States. Slater Mill, built in 1793, was the nation's first water-powered cotton mill. Within a generation, more than 150 mills were operating in the area.

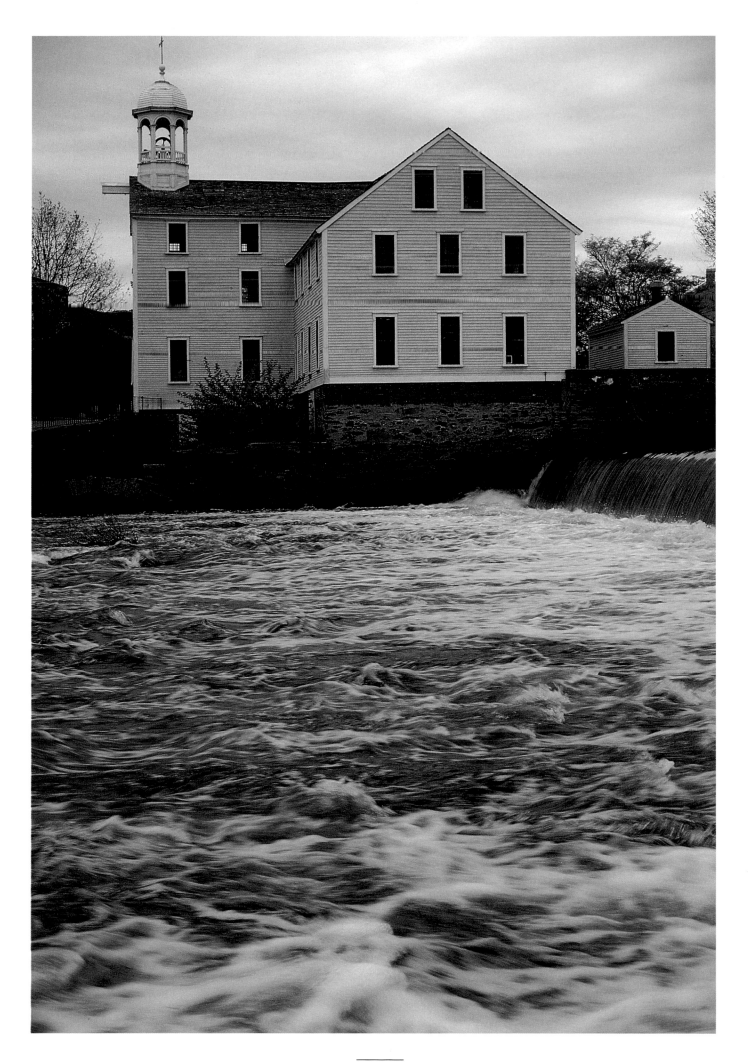

*I fully and conscientiously believe
that it is the will of the Almighty
that there should be diversity
of religious opinions among us.*
THOMAS PAINE

◄ In Little Compton, Rhode Island, gravestones of early colonists such as John Alden's daughter dot the Old Burying Ground adjacent to the United Congregational church. A headstone near those of Mr. and Mrs. Simeon Palmer bears the intriguing message, "In memory of Elisabeth, who should have been the wife of Mr. Simeon Palmer, who died August 14, 1776, in the 64th year of her age." Rhode Island, the smallest state in the nation, is known as the "Ocean State," and although it measures only thirty-eight miles in a straight east/west line, it has more than four hundred miles of coast.

▲ On New Year's Day, hardy citizens of Narragansett Pier brave 40° water in the "Pier Plunge" to raise money for charity. Along with grand hotels, the grand pier, which existed when the town was a nineteenth-century watering place, was destroyed by a fire in 1900.

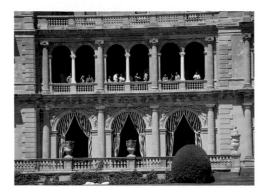

Newport, Rhode Island, has a varied visual history. Its beautiful location on an island in Narragansett Bay has for centuries attracted sea lovers. In Newport's Gilded Age, at the end of the nineteenth century, magnificent "cottages" were built here by some of the nation's wealthiest families. *The Breakers,* erected for Cornelius Vanderbilt II and containing seventy opulent rooms, was patterned after a Renaissance Italian palace. Contemporary mansions are now background for a working lobster boat on Ocean Drive. During the American Revolution, Newport was occupied and ravished by the British Army. Today, colorful revolutionary reenactments use costumed militia such as these on the steps of Colony House.

◄ "The State of Rhode Island and Providence Plantations" is the name of this tiny state. The two-mile-long Newport Bridge connects Newport, on Rhode Island, with Jamestown, on Conanicut Island.
▲ Trinity Church, built in the style of English architect Christopher Wren, towers above Queen Anne Square facing Newport's active waterfront. A "wineglass" pulpit set on three levels is a unique feature of the church. The Common, or Green, is a familiar sight in New England towns. Commons were used for community livestock grazing as well as for militia drills. Today, Commons serve contemporary towns as parks and gathering places.

Mystic, Connecticut, houses and preserves its shipbuilding and whaling heritage in the re-created outdoor museum at Mystic Seaport. The only survivor of the nineteenth-century whaling fleet, the *Charles W. Morgan* is docked at the Mystic River waterfront. The *Morgan*, 111 feet in length, was equipped to carry more than twenty-seven hundred barrels of whale oil. Costumed crafts-people demonstrate traditional seafaring activities in the sail loft, the "ropewalk," and in many stores and workshops.

◄ History and progress meet as the ultramodern People's Bank and the flamboyant Barnum Museum jockey for the eye in Bridgeport, Connecticut. Phineas T. Barnum, creator of the circus billed as "The Greatest Show on Earth," designed this fantastic, fanciful building.
▲ New London, like "old" London, is situated on the banks of the Thames River, but in true independent New England fashion, here it is pronounced "Thaymes," not "Temms"! The United States Coast Guard Academy is based in New London. In 1781, redcoats, led by the traitorous Benedict Arnold and looking much like the members of this fife and drum corps, laid waste to the settlement which had served as a patriot privateer base.

▲ The Indians named Connecticut "beside the long tidal river." The broad Connecticut River courses more than four hundred miles from its source in northern New Hampshire. Often compared in beauty to the Rhine, this river even has its own castle, built by Shakespearean actor, William Gillette. Pastoral countryside persists in the valley because sandbars at the mouth of the river have prevented the development found along other major American rivers.
▶ Lying within the ring of New York City suburbs, Norwalk has a manufacturing past intermingled with ties to the sea. The Maritime Center at Norwalk includes an aquarium, various hands-on nautical exhibits, and educational displays of Long Island Sound marine life.

◄ Sixteen Norwalk islands speckle the mouth of the Norwalk River on Long Island Sound. Each has had unique uses. Chimon Island, part of the McKinney National Wildlife Refuge, has no permanent human population. This seventy-acre wilderness environment, located just over a mile from a teeming megalopolis, is habitat for Connecticut's largest nesting colony of herons, egrets, and ibises.

▲ Three of the hundreds of egrets hatched on Chimon Island early each summer wait hungrily for breakfast. Two rangers camp on the island for several days each week to catalog bird behavior and count population in this crowded rookery.

There is something magnificent in having a country to love . . .
JAMES RUSSELL LOWELL

▲ Stamford, hometown to many of America's large corporations, offers a rich cultural life. This vibrant Connecticut city, with its Long Island Sound harbor, owes much of its successful growth to its proximity to New York City, here visible some thirty miles away.
▶ In celebration of its three hundred fiftieth birthday, the town of Greenwich—the "Gateway to New England"—raises the world's largest American flag. In a park at the edge of Greenwich Harbor, as some five thousand townspeople look on, the huge "Mount Rushmore" flag is lifted slowly from the arms of the descendants of the town's original settlers. Love of country, pride in the past, reverence for tradition, community spirit—each Yankee characteristic is symbolized in this New England Coast event.

AFTERWORD

Books like this do not just happen. Though I am listed as "author," this project involved the input of scores of people who deserve recognition. First is Donna Callighan, my studio manager, who has now worked with me on this, our fourth book project. Captioning, filing, and computerizing thousands of slides is a job she has done superbly. My thanks next go to the more than fifty people who responded to my questionnaire that guided me in where and what to photograph up and down the New England Coast.

Also to be remembered are the Chambers of Commerce who were kind enough to keep me on their mailing lists, as well as the public relations offices at Mystic Seaport, Strawbery Banke, the U.S. Coast Guard Academy, Norwalk Maritime Center, and many others. A special thanks to Paul Casey of the National Wildlife Service.

Then there are the friends who offered their hospitality up and down our forty-five hundred miles of coastline. Kitty and Dick Pierson, Alice and George Wallis, Winifred Clark, Nat and Holly Pulsifer, Anne and Dick Wright, Nancy and Bill Easman, Trina and Rob Greene, Esu and Dan Lackey, Joanne Ball and Bill Fontana, and Cathy Christ-Janer.

Finally, special thanks and love go to my wife, Jeannie, for her unflagging energy and support in this project. This book has been a joyous joint venture. We hope the fun we have had in producing NEW ENGLAND COAST will stimulate you to explore it for yourself.

WILLIAM HUBBELL